Beginning VOLLEYBALL

Thanks to Coach Lynne McDonald and the following members of the Mosquito Coast Volleyball Club:
  Charleen Anderson,
  Rebecca Bauer,
  Heather Canonico,
  Deanna Foss,
  Jill Gowling,
  Sarah Runka,
  Christina Rybak,
  Lisa Shanblott,
and coaches Bob Stanek and José Jones, and the following members of the Team 'Sota Volleyball Club:
  Tim Dougherty,
  Lester Drankwalter,
  Brad Johnson,
  Flynn McKeegan,
  Danny Seppala,
  Pat Smith,
  Adam Southwick,
  and David Westbrook,
who were photographed for this book.

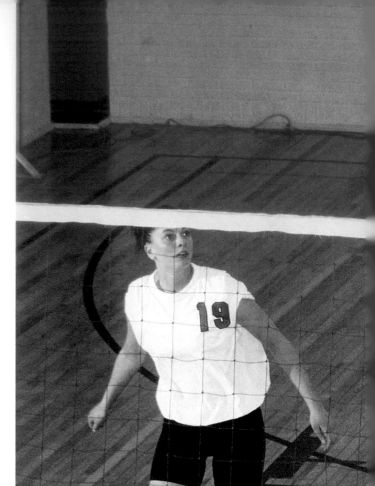

Beginning
VOLLEYBALL

Julie Jensen

Adapted from *Fundamental Volleyball*

Photographs by Andy King

Lerner Publications Company ● Minneapolis

To Larry and Dave

Library of Congress Cataloging-in-Publication Data

Jensen, Julie, 1957-
    Beginning Volleyball/by Julie Jensen ; adapted from
Fundamental Volleyball ; photographs by Andy King.
        p.   cm. — (Beginning sports)
    Includes bibliographical references and index.
    ISBN 0–8225–3502–5 :
    1. Volleyball—Juvenile literature. [1. Volleyball] I. King,
Andy, ill. II. Jensen, Julie, 1957-   Fundamental Volleyball.
III. Title. IV. Series.
GV1015.3.J46   1995
796.325—dc20   94–29509
                                                         CIP
                                                          AC

Manufactured in the United States of America

1 2 3 4 5 - I/HP - 99 98 97 96 95

Photo Acknowledgments

Photographs are reproduced with the permission of: p. 7, Gerry Vuchetich, University of Minnesota Women's Intercollegiate Athletics; p. 8 (both), Volleyball Hall of Fame; pp. 9, 49, @ Allsport USA/Bruce Hazelton, 1984; pp. 13, 27, 56, United States Volleyball Association; p. 57, Richard Kane/SportsChrome East/West; p. 58, Florida Department of Commerce, Division of Tourism.

Contents

Chapter 1

How This Game Got Started

Volleyball is a game of nonstop motion. The ball must be kept moving. Players don't catch and throw the ball to each other. Instead, they bounce or pass it to teammates and hit it over the net at opponents.

William G. Morgan invented volleyball at his Holyoke, Massachusetts, gymnasium in 1895. Morgan was the physical fitness director at the local Young Men's

College volleyball players, like Sue Jackson of the University of Minnesota team, make the games fun to watch.

7

Christian Association (YMCA). He wanted to combine some of the skills of baseball, handball, and tennis into a new sport. Morgan (pictured at left) told the players to use their hands to bat the ball back and forth over the net.

Now most high schools have volleyball teams for girls. Some offer the game for boys also. About 1,200 colleges have women's teams. Some 60 colleges

have men's teams. Many people play at YMCAs and recreation centers.

The United States Volleyball Association (USVBA) organizes teams and tournaments. In 1993, the USVBA had about 93,000 members. The USVBA also runs the Junior Olympics Program for players ages 10 to 18. Some 48,000 young athletes played in USVBA tournaments in 1993.

The USVBA also helps sponsor the U.S. Olympic teams. Every four years, at the Summer Olympic Games, the best volleyball teams in the world compete for a gold medal.

This book will introduce you to the basics of volleyball. Just as in any sport, learning to play volleyball takes time and effort. If you are patient and persistent, you can become a good volleyball player—maybe even an Olympian.

Gold in 1984

Volleyball was invented in the United States, but athletes in other countries quickly learned the sport. Players in Japan, China, Cuba, and the former Soviet Union became very good at volleyball. Teams from these countries were the best in the world.

The United States had never won an Olympic gold medal in volleyball until 1984. The U.S. men's team began the Olympic Games with three victories, but Brazil defeated the Americans 15-12, 15-11, 15-2 in their fourth match of the Olympics.

Five nights later, the Americans were in the gold-medal final. They defeated the Brazilian team 15-6, 15-6, 15-7, to win America's first gold medal in volleyball. The U.S. men won the gold medal again in 1988.

Chapter 2

BASICS

Just like tennis and basketball, volleyball is played on a court. The court is 29 feet, 6 inches wide and 59 feet long. A net is strung across the middle of the court. The net is usually more than 7 feet high. Sometimes the net is lower for beginners.

The **center line** is directly under the net. There are also lines on each side of the net. These lines are about 10 feet away from the net. They are called the **10-foot lines,** or **attack lines.**

The Ball

A volleyball weighs about 9 ounces and is about 26 inches around.

11

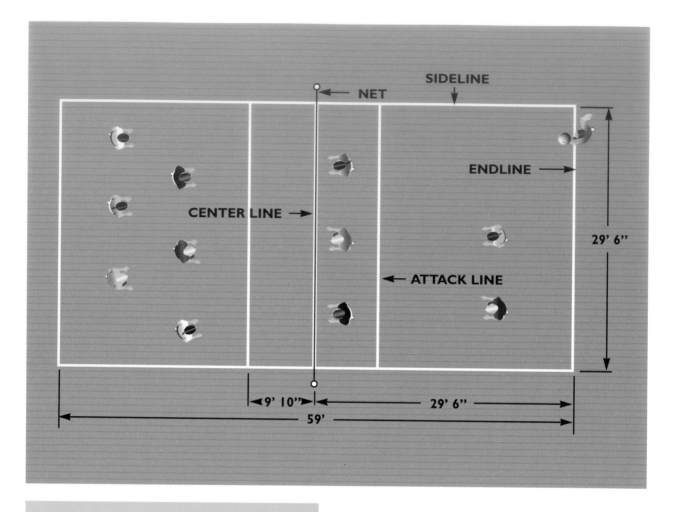

SIDELINE

NET

ENDLINE

CENTER LINE →

29' 6"

← ATTACK LINE

9' 10"

29' 6"

59'

Faults

Volleyball rules keep the game fair. Some violations of the rules are:

- *touching the net at any time*
- *stepping on the endline while serving*
- *stepping on the center line*
- *catching or throwing the ball*
- *hitting the ball more than three times on a side*
- *serving when it isn't your turn*
- *a player hitting the ball two times in a row*

Rules

Each team has six players. The object of the game is to use your hands or forearms to hit the ball over the net so that it lands in the opponent's playing area. A team tries to prevent the ball from hitting the floor in its own area.

Play starts with a **serve**. One player hits the ball directly over the net into the other team's court. If the ball touches the net, the other team gets to serve.

Only the serving team can score points. If the ball hits the floor on the receiving team's side, the serving team scores one point.

If the ball hits the floor on the serving team's court, the receiving team gets to serve. The players on that team then **rotate,** or move clockwise one position. The player in the right back position serves.

A game is played until one team scores 15 points. The winning team must have at least two more points than its opponent. If the score is 15 to 14, the game goes on until one team has two more points than the other. A series of games makes up a **match.** To win a match, a team must win two of three games or three of five games.

Players are either front row players or back row players. Front row players usually play between the attack line and the net. Back row players defend the back area of the court.

Any player may pass or set the ball. Only players in the front row positions may spike or block it.

Calling the Game

In school or USVBA games, five officials make sure all the rules are followed. Sometimes, in recreational play, only one official is used.

*The **first referee** is in charge of the match. He or she stands on a ladder at one end of the net. The first referee signals for the players to serve.*

*The **second referee** stands on the floor at the other end of the net. She or he watches to make sure no players touch the net.*

*A **scorekeeper** keeps track of the score and timeouts at a table near the court. The two **line judges,** at opposite corners of the court, signal if a ball is hit in the court or if it is out.*

The Team 'Sota boys and the Mosquito Coast girls will demonstrate volleyball's basic moves.

Serving

Charleen and her Mosquito Coast teammates are practicing their serves. There are several ways to serve. Two common serves are underhand and overhand.

Charleen is hitting an **underhand serve**. She holds the ball in one hand. Then, while stepping forward, she gently tosses the ball in the air, swings her other arm forward, and hits the ball from below with her fist.

Charleen has to be sure that the ball goes over the net and lands within the court area. By changing her aim, Charleen can hit the ball to different places on the court.

If Charleen hits the ball too hard or off to the side, her serve will land outside the playing area. When her serve lands out of bounds, Charleen's team loses the serve. Then the other team gets to serve.

Clothing

Most people wear T-shirts and shorts or sweatpants when playing volleyball. Wear gym shoes when you play so you can jump and run. Many players wear knee pads to protect their knees.

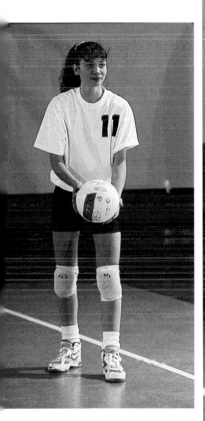

To hit an **overhand serve**, Charleen tosses the ball up in the air slightly in front of her head. Her other hand is pulled back behind her head. As the ball comes down, Charleen swings her arm forward. She hits the center of the ball with her open hand when the ball is just above her head.

Think Positively

Before you serve, imagine yourself tossing up the ball, hitting it, and watching it go over the net and in. Some players believe that imagining a good serve helps them serve correctly. You can do this for many sports activities, such as making a free throw in basketball or serving in tennis. Just remember, open your eyes before you take your shot!

Passing

Players **pass** the ball to each other to set up a strong hit. To do the **forearm pass**, Jill links her hands with her thumbs together. She keeps her arms out away from her body. Her knees are bent. Jill tries to hit the ball with her forearms when the ball is about waist high. This pass is also called a bump pass.

If the ball is hit softly over to their side of the court, the Mosquitoes use the **overhead pass**.

Christina stands with her knees bent. Her arms are above her head. Her elbows are bent and her fingers are spread wide open. She watches the ball through her fingers.

Once the ball touches her hands, Christina guides the ball toward the ceiling and forward. After the ball has touched her hands, she extends her fingers forward in a straight line. That is her **follow-through**. Following through helps the ball go where Christina aims it.

Setting

A **set** is a special kind of overhead pass that is used to set up a scoring attempt. A teammate passes the ball to the setter. Then, the setter sends a soft, easy pass—a set—to the hitter to hit over the net.

Danny is setting. He stands with his side to the net. He quickly moves underneath the pass. Danny uses an overhead pass to set. He wants to put the ball about 5 feet higher than the net and about 2 feet from it.

Spiking

Spiking is volleyball's version of basketball's slam dunk. A hitter slams the ball over the net and down on the other side of the court for a **spike**.

When Danny starts to set the ball, Brad quickly takes several running steps—his **approach**— toward the net. Then he stops with both feet together.

Brad jumps straight up. The running start helps Brad jump high enough to hit the ball when it is above the net.

At the top of his jump, Brad hits the ball with an open hand. The ball is above his head and slightly in front of him. Brad swings his arm forward as he follows through. He is careful not to touch the net.

Flo Hyman's Spiking Legacy

Flo Hyman was one of the best spikers in American volleyball history. She was a 6-foot, 5-inch hitter on the U.S. Olympic team that finished second in the 1984 Olympics. That was the best the American women had ever done in the Olympics.

Flo said winning the silver medal was one of the proudest moments of her life. But it took her nine years of hard work on the U.S. team to achieve this goal.

The United States hadn't won a spot in the Olympics since women's volleyball had become an Olympic sport in 1964. Flo and a group of U.S. women began working toward that goal in 1974.

Flo and her teammates qualified for the 1980 Olympic Games. But the trip to the Games was not to be. President Jimmy Carter ordered all American athletes to stay away from the Olympics because the Games were being held in the Soviet Union. President Carter wanted to protest the Soviet Union's war with Afghanistan.

Flo and six of her teammates continued to practice and wait for the 1984 Olympics. Those Games were scheduled to be in Los Angeles.

Flo kept improving. In 1981 she was named the world's best hitter. Her five sisters and two brothers could hardly believe she was the same person who had been too shy and scared to try out for her high school team as a 14-year-old.

Finally 1984 arrived. Flo and the U.S. team went into the Games with high hopes. They had worked hard for a long time. They were a good team. But the Chinese team was better. After a thrilling match, China won the gold medal.

Flo was proud of her silver medal, though. She decided that she could leave the U.S. national team. She went to Japan, where businesses paid players to play volleyball. Volleyball had always been her love, and Flo liked having it as her job too.

In Japan, while playing a volleyball game, Flo Hyman died. She was 31 years old and very fit. But she had a heart condition she didn't even know about, called Marfan's syndrome. It caused her heart to stop beating.

Each year, the Women's Sports Foundation honors Flo Hyman's memory by giving an award to a young, female athlete.

Blocking

Lisa is **blocking,** or trying to prevent the other team's spiker from hitting the ball to her side of the court. Blockers have to be careful not to touch the net.

Lisa stands across from where the ball will be hit. She jumps straight up and spreads her fingers as wide as she can. She tries to touch the ball and make it fall back on the spiker's side.

Defense

If the ball gets past the blocker,
the rest of the team must be
ready for it. Good defensive players figure out where the ball will
land. They move quickly to get
under it.

Heather bends her legs and
stays low to the floor so she can
dive for balls. Heather tries to
use both of her forearms to pass
the ball.

But sometimes Heather has to really stretch to make a pass. That is called a **dig**. Heather gets only one arm or fist under the ball. She hits the ball with her fist or the heel of her hand. She tries to direct the ball toward the middle of her court, to where a teammate can set it.

Digs and other difficult passes are called **saves**. Saves can be as exciting as spikes.

Chapter 3

GAME TIME

The Mosquito Coast team will be playing in a tournament. To get ready for it, Coach McDonald splits the team into two squads for a practice game. Coach McDonald will coach the Skeeters. Coach Shelley will coach the Coasters. The two coaches will also act as referees.

The Skeeters serve first. Barb's overhand serve is a good one. It goes over the net without touching it.

The Coasters have trouble passing Barb's serve. Instead of spiking the ball to the Skeeters' side of the court, the Coasters bump it over.

Now the Skeeters are ready to try to score a point. Coach McDonald has told the Skeeters that she wants them to use all three of their hits: pass, set, spike.

Janai passes to Sarah, who sets the ball for Maura. Maura

spikes the ball. It goes over the net and lands in the Coasters' court. The Skeeters are on the scoreboard!

On the next play a Coaster spiker jumps up to hit the ball. Charleen blocks the ball back over the net. But the ball lands outside the court. Since Charleen last touched the ball before it landed out of bounds, the Coasters will now serve.

Winning the serve is called a sideout. After a **sideout,** the team about to serve must rotate. The players move clockwise one position. The new right back player serves.

Usually a back row player returns the serve, so Kristi, Janai,

and Barb are on their toes.

The serve goes nearest to Janai, who runs to pass it. The ball bounces wildly off her arms and hits the ceiling. The Coasters have scored a point.

Janai shuffles her feet nervously. She thinks the Coaster server will hit the ball to her again. She's right.

This time, the ball bounces cleanly off of Janai's arms and over the net. No bump-set-spike this time for the Skeeters. Now they must play defense.

The Coaster spiker hits the ball and Kristi dives with her

arms outstretched. The ball hits her arms and pops up. Sarah passes it to Maura, who hits the ball over. It bounces off of a Coasters' back row player and lands far outside the court. Side-out for the Skeeters.

Maura serves and the Coasters return the ball with a crunching spike. The ball shoots between the Skeeters' blockers. It lands inbounds on the Skeeters' side. Now the Coasters will serve.

The Coaster's serve fools the

Skeeters. At first, Kristi thinks it's heading for her, but then it seems to move toward Jill. Kristi thinks Jill is going to handle the ball. Jill thinks Kristi is. The ball lands on the floor between them. The Coasters have won another point.

Coach McDonald calls for a timeout. The Skeeters huddle around their coach. She tells the Skeeters, "Remember to call for the ball. Don't wait for a teammate to take it. Call out 'Mine' and then pass it. Let's go."

On the next serve, Kristi yells "Mine" and passes the ball to the front row. Sarah sets the ball to Charleen, who hits it down on the Coaster side. Now the Skeeters are on the right track.

Passing Primer

To be a good passer, remember:
- *Watch the ball until it hits your arms.*
- *Bend your knees to keep your balance.*
- *Aim the ball toward your target.*

Much later in the game, the Skeeters are ahead, 14-13. If the Skeeters win the next point, they win the game.

But Maura's serve goes into the net. The Coasters score on their serve to tie the game at 14-14. Then the Skeeters get a sideout. Now they have to score two points to win.

Sarah's serve is a fast one. A Coaster back row player bumps the ball over the net.

Sarah passes the ball to Kristi. Janai calls "Yes" to let Kristi know she's ready to spike the ball. Kristi gently sets the ball out to Janai. Janai jumps and swings her arm as fast as she can. Thwack. The ball lands on the Coasters' court for a Skeeter point.

Sarah is serving. More than anything, she wants to make sure her serve is good. She imagines the ball going over the net and landing on the other side.

Coach McDonald signals Sarah to serve. Sarah takes a deep breath. Then she tosses up the ball and hits it solidly. The ball goes over the net.

But the Coasters are able to set the ball up to one of their hitters. When the spiker is about to hit the ball, Janai springs up, fingers spread wide. The Coaster spiker hits the ball into Janai's hands. The ball bounces back over the net and falls to the floor in the Coasters' court. The Skeeters win!

Chapter 4

PRACTICE, PRACTICE

There are fun drills players can practice to improve their volleyball skills. Better skills will make the games more fun too.

Conditioning

Volleyball players must be able to play long games without losing their energy. Running increases endurance and stamina, so Coach Stanek has his players jog in place before practice.

When the players are sweaty and warmed up, they stretch their muscles. Stretching helps them become more flexible.

Volleyball players also should be able to jump just as high at the end of a match as they can at the beginning. For that, they need strong leg muscles. Jumping up and down strengthens those muscles. Jumping rope does too.

To strengthen his finger muscles, Danny makes tight fists and then opens his fingers wide. He also squeezes tennis balls to build up muscles for setting.

Drills

The Team 'Sota players are practicing their serves. They put a chair on each side of the court. Players serve from both ends of the court. They try to hit the chair opposite them with their serves.

Passing is another skill that Team 'Sota players work on often. This drill keeps them moving.

Half of the players line up, one behind the other. The other players line up facing them. The lines are about 10 feet apart.

David tosses the ball to Bob, then runs and stands at the end of Bob's line. Bob passes the ball to Kris. Then Bob goes to the end of Kris's line. The players continue passing and following their pass until the ball hits the floor.

The players must control their passes to keep the ball moving. As they get better, the two lines move farther apart.

Sarah and her teammates also practice passing. In this drill, Coach McDonald hits the ball to Sarah. Sarah passes the ball to a teammate at the net. Then Sarah goes to the net to catch a pass from the next passer.

In another drill, Coach Stanek hits the ball to one player, who passes the ball. The passer sends the ball to another player, the setter, who sets the ball. After a third player, the hitter, has hit the ball over, the players switch positions.

Everyone loves to practice spiking. In this drill, Sarah stands near the net to set the ball. The other girls stand in a line. The first girl in line tosses the ball to Sarah. Sarah sets the ball for the tosser, who spikes it over. Then it is the next girl's turn.

Charleen, Lisa, and Deanna are playing "pepper." Charleen tosses the ball to Lisa. She passes or sets the ball to Deanna, who hits or sets the ball back to Charleen. They try to keep the ball from hitting the floor for as long as possible.

If she's alone, Charleen plays pepper against the wall. She hits the ball so that it bounces on the floor first. Then the ball bounces off the wall and back to her. Since the wall never misses, Charleen would rather play with Lisa!

For this fast-paced drill, the Team 'Sota players get into teams of three. Coach Stanek hits the ball to one of the teams. Two teams play out a point. The team that loses the point leaves the court. Another team quickly replaces it.

Chapter 5

RAZZLE DAZZLE

When they watch high school and college matches, Danny, Sarah, and their teammates see some tricky moves. The players work on these advanced skills in practice.

Jump Serve

Becky is practicing her favorite move, the **jump serve**. The jump serve takes lots of work.

Jump Serving Star

Karch Kiraly (kur-EYE) was one of the first American players to make the jump serve popular. He is a versatile player who passes and spikes very well. But many fans like his jump serve the best. Karch's special flair is tossing the ball up with one hand while the other is on his hip.

Karch and teammate Steve Timmons led the U.S. men to two Olympic gold medals. Karch was named the Most Valuable Player in the 1988 Olympics. Karch makes a living by playing beach volleyball.

Becky begins her jump serve by holding the ball with both hands. Then she throws the ball up above her head and in front of her. She jumps and hits the ball, just like for a spike. But Becky can jump forward without worrying about hitting the net.

Tips

Sometimes a spiker lightly taps the ball over the net instead of spiking it. Because the defenders are expecting a hard hit, they aren't ready for a soft shot. These shots are called **tips**, or **dinks**. Deanna keeps her wrist and elbow locked when she practices tipping. Just her fingertips flick the ball over.

Back Sets

Danny works on **back sets** at every practice. A back set starts out just like a regular set. But when Danny touches the ball, he pushes it over his head and back instead of in front of him. At the same time, he pushes his hips forward and arches his back. His follow-through is up and back. This motion sends the ball behind him. A good back set will fool the other team's blockers.

Chapter 6

MORE WAYS TO PLAY

There are many ways to play volleyball. Some people use four players on a team. One player stands by the net, two side players are halfway down the sidelines, and a back player is in the middle of the endline. Only the front three players can spike and block.

Players might also play with three to a side. This is called triples. The player in the middle stays by the net to block and set. The other two players pass the ball and spike. The players still rotate before they serve.

Another variation is doubles, with two players on each side. Players take turns serving. Both players pass, set, and spike.

Barbra Fontana (opposite page) and Karch Kiraly (above) play pro beach volleyball.

57

Many people play volleyball on the beach. It takes a little practice to play on the sand in bare feet. Beach volleyball is so popular that some men and women are professional beach volleyball players. They play in tournaments for prize money.

People also play volleyball on grass, in backyards or parks. There are lots of places to play volleyball. Ask the gym teacher at your school about places to play. Or stop in at a recreation center or community playground close to your home and ask.

Junior high schools and high schools often have volleyball teams. Some high school players receive scholarships to play on college volleyball teams. A few players who are very talented play on the Olympic team or in professional leagues. You could be one of them.

Or you may enjoy playing in a rec center with your friends. Either way, knowing the right moves makes volleyball a fun sport for a lifetime.

VOLLEYBALL TALK

approach: A series of quick, running steps a hitter takes before spiking the ball.

attack line: A line about 3 meters, or 10 feet, from the net.

back set: A set that goes behind the setter's head.

block: To try to prevent the other team's spike from coming across the net by jumping up and letting the ball hit your hands.

center line: The line on the court directly beneath the net.

dig: A return or pass of a hard-hit ball.

dink: A gentle hit after jumping as if to spike it; also called a **tip**.

fault: An illegal move or play.

first referee: The official in charge of the match; stands on a ladder or small platform at one end of the net.

follow through: To continue a motion after contacting the ball.

forearm pass: A hit with straight forearms in front of your body; also called a bump pass.

jump serve: A serve in which the server tosses the ball and then jumps to hit it.

line judge: The official who watches to see where the ball lands. Usually, there are two line judges for a game.

match: A series of games played between two teams. The first team to win two games in a three-game match or three games in a five-game match wins the match.

overhand serve: A serve in which the server tosses the ball and hits it when it is above his or her head but doesn't jump to hit it.

overhead pass: A pass made by contacting the ball with only the fingertips and directing it to a teammate.

pass: To hit the ball to a teammate, either with an overhead pass or a forearm pass.

rotate: To move one position clockwise.

save: To keep the ball from hitting the floor, usually with a dive or dig.

scorekeeper: The official who keeps track of how many points each team has during a game.

second referee: The official who stands on the floor at one end of the net.

serve: To put the ball in play by hitting it directly over the net and into the other team's court.

set: To put the ball in position for a teammate to hit it over the net.

sideout: Winning the chance to serve.

spike: To forcefully hit the ball over the net.

10-foot line: Line about 3 meters, or 10 feet, from the net; also called **attack line**.

tip: To gently hit the ball over the net after jumping as if to spike it; also called a **dink**.

underhand serve: A serve in which the server tosses the ball and hits it by swinging his or her arm forward below the waist.

FURTHER READING

Bertucci, Bob. *Championship Volley-ball: By the Experts.* West Point, New York: Leisure Press, 1982.

Egstrom, Glen H., and Frances Schaafsma. *Volleyball.* Wm. C. Brown Publishers, 1984.

Kiraly, Karch. *Karch Kiraly's Championship Volleyball.* New York: Simon & Schuster Inc., 1990.

Lucas, Jeff. *Pass, Set, Crush: Volleyball Illustrated.* Euclid Northwest Publications, 1988.

Lyttle, Richard. *Basic Volleyball Techniques.* Garden City, New York: Double-day, 1979.

Scates, Allen E. *Winning Volleyball.* Newton, Massachusetts: Allyn and Bacon, Inc., 1984.

FOR MORE INFORMATION

United States Volleyball Association
3595 East Fountain Boulevard
Colorado Springs, CO 80910

INDEX